The Unofficial

HEARTLAND

Cookbook

Mike Hurley and Nita Abbott

Text and photographs copyright © 2022 Nita Abbott.

Published in the United States of America
ISBN: 9798353450146
Printed in the United States of America
Interior Book Design: Katherine Watkins
Front Cover Design: Al Saker
Subjects: Cooking, Canadian. Cooking, American

This book is an independent fan publication. No endorsement, license, or affiliation with Working Partners, Olympia Films, Seven24Films or CBC or any of their affiliates is claimed. Copyrighted or trademarked characters and other elements of the Heartland show that are referenced in this book are the property of their respective owners and are used for informational and transformative purposes only.

Many of the designations used by manufacturers and sellers to distinguish their products are claimed as trademarks. Where those designations appear in this book is at all, if the authors and their publisher were aware of a trademark claim, the designations have been printed in capital letters at the beginning of each word.

Always follow safety and common sense cooking protocols while using kitchen utensils, operating ovens and stoves and handling uncooked food. If children are assisting in the preparation of any recipe, they should always be supervised by an adult.

For Our families, both Human and Animal

Contents

Forward • 1

Chapter 1: Breakfast • 3

Chapter 2: Appetizers & Sides • 17

Contents

Chapter 3: Main Dishes • 33

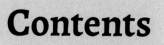

Contents

Chapter 4: Desserts & Beverages • 93

About the Author • 117
US/Metric Conversion Chart • 118

Forward

If you're a fan of the hit Canadian TV series Heartland, you know almost every episode has at least one meal shared in it. Food is a common denominator for many millions of families all around the world. Thankfully, Jack Bartlett knows the value of bringing his family together around the dinner table. Maybe you've eaten dinner while watching Heartland. Pass the rolls please! Now your family can enjoy some of the same foods as the characters eat on the show. Who can forget Time for Tim's pancakes or Mrs. Bell's Award Winning Jam? Remember Grandpa Jack's date with Lisa where he made her a tasty fish fry? Lisa was impressed to find out Jack could cook, a redeeming quality in a cowboy.

From a campfire to a crockpot, Jack Bartlett can wrangle up some of the best grub you've ever had. Now cowboys don't carry measuring spoons, but Jack cooks enough to know that a pinch of salt is about 1/6 of a teaspoon. In this book you'll find such recipes as Grandpa Jack's Beef Stew which will be sure to stick to your ribs to such exotic items as Lou's forays into Vegan cooking for her boyfriend Mitch's girlfriend (don't ask) and her special Dinner of Dubai from her travels with Peter to the Middle East.

Food begins to play an even bigger role in Heartland as Heartland family starts to grow and Lou buys the only diner in Hudson, Maggie's. Mallory even had her first solid food at Maggie's, their famous Poutine French Fries! I myself am a home cook who has been enamored with Heartland for years to the extent that I write serious Heartland fanfiction, and I am so delighted to be a part of this project that is sure to put a smile on the face of anyone who reads it, and especially anyone who tries one of our fun and delectable recipes. After sending Amber Marshall my home grown honey for years (I'm an amateur beekeeper) I hope readers will appreciate the sweet honey taste in some of the recipes I have contributed to this cookbook.

I know readers are going to love this Heartland cookbook, so many memories of the show have been stirred into yummy Heartland recipes. So make Mrs. Bell's Award Winning Jam, or Grandpa Jack's Alberta Burgers or one of Maggie's Sweet And Creamy Milkshakes and if you're feeling ultra adventurous try your hand at Lisa's Five Alarm Venison Stew or Caleb's Beer Steak. Then after you've made your Heartland meal pull up a chair and fill your plate and watch Heartland. The whole Heartland clan is welcoming you in for a delicious meal, in a home where everyone is welcome it's like you are part of the family! Enjoy!!

—Mike Hurley

CHAPTER 1:
BREAKFAST

Time for Tim's Political Pancakes

Tim might often seem self-serving and a bit rude, but when he was running for President of the Cowboy Association he went out of his way to be as nice as he could possibly be-to would be voters that is! Luckily for him, serving the voters these scrumptious melt in your mouth fluffy pancakes might have been his best idea yet! These authentic Canadian pancakes, which are fluffier than American pancakes and should be made with Canadian flour, because it is self rising and makes the pancakes light and fluffy. But if you can't find Canadian flour, use King Arthur self rising baking flour as it is most similar to Canadian flour. Also, to get these pancakes as fluffy as possible be sure to beat the egg whites and yolk separately. Though Tim didn't win his bid for President of the Cowboy Association of Hudson, he certainly couldn't have helped but impress the voters with these light fluffy Canadian Pancakes!

Makes 8 Pancakes

Ingredients:

- 1 cup Canadian flour, or King Arthur's baking flour
- 1 Tablespoon baking powder
- 1 cup Milk
- 2 egg yolks

- 3 egg whites
- 1 teaspoon vanilla extract
- 2 teaspoon white sugar
- Pinch of salt

1. In a large bowl combine the flour and baking powder. Stir in the milk and egg yolks until smooth. In another large bowl beat the egg whites until they are stiff or at least foamy.

2. Fold a little bit of the egg whites into the batter, stir then mix the rest in. Don't over-stir once you mix the egg whites in.

3. Heat an oiled frying pan over medium high heat and make pancakes of a desired size. For 8 pancakes use ¼ cup of batter per pancake. Pancakes should be flipped when you see a few bubbles in the middle of the batter of each, and then cooked until light golden brown.

Marnie's Huevos Rancheros

Marnie might be one of Lou's oldest and best friends-after all they have known each other since grade school-but just like everyone else in Lou's life, their relationship is often complicated.

Having an anxious and competitive personality like Lou has does not lend itself to having easy relationships! Luckily for Lou though, Marnie is easy going and always willing to lend Lou a helping hand. Since Marnie is a local caterer in Hudson, Lou turns to Marnie when Lou has nothing to make for her first dude ranch guests for breakfast. With Marnie's skillful help Lou is able to come up with this delicious South of the Border inspired recipe that wows her picky guests, and this southwest special recipe is sure to wow you as well!

Serves 4, or 2 really hungry Dude Ranch guests!

Ingredients:

- ½ cup onion, chopped
- ½ cup bell pepper, chopped
- ½ cup tomato, chopped
- 2 cloves of garlic, finely chopped
- 4 eggs
- 4 tortillas

- ½ cup cheddar cheese, shredded
- Pinch of cayenne pepper
- Pinch of salt
- Pinch of black pepper
- optional : Sour cream and salsa to taste

1. Fry the onions first in a large frying pan, until they just turn slightly brown, then add the garlic, bell pepper and tomatoes and cook for an additional five minutes.

2. Next crack the 4 eggs and add them to the pan being careful not to break the egg yolks. Cover the pan and poach the eggs until the egg whites are done, about 3 minutes.

3. Uncover and place the shredded cheese on top. Meanwhile, warm the tortillas for 30 seconds in the microwave. Put one egg and some of the cheesy vegetable mixture on top of each tortilla and sprinkle a little cayenne pepper, salt and black pepper on top to taste. Add salsa and sour cream to taste as well.

Maggie's Rancher's Breakfast Special

The rancher's breakfast special at Maggie's is a favorite with the Heartland family and many other Hudson locals. The heavy protein laden part of the special sat well with ranchers who might only have this one meal to tide them over until they go back home at nightfall after a long day of watching their cattle and other livestock like Jack and Tim. Of course, Tim being Tim he always makes Jack or Caleb pay for his meal!

Serves 1

Ingredients:

- 2 eggs
- 3 slices of Canadian bacon
- 4 pieces of SteakUms
- 1 piece of sliced cheddar cheese

1. In a large frying pan place the 2 slices of Canadian bacon and cook until the bacon starts to curl at the edges. Transfer the bacon to a breakfast plate.

2. Using the grease from the bacon, fry 4 pieces of SteakUms in the pan until the pieces are no longer pink and transfer to the breakfast plate.

3. Next crack 2 eggs being careful not to break the yolks. Fry the eggs to desired doneness (but you know Jack likes his sunny side up and Tim likes his sunny side down!) and transfer to a breakfast plate.

4. Last place a ½ slice of cheddar cheese on top of the eggs.

Lou's Coronaries in a Basket Cinnamon Rolls

Lou might be a serious businesswoman but that doesn't mean she doesn't dabble in domestic pursuits like baking-especially when those baked goods will attract more customers to her business at the dude ranch. So she is more than happy to bake cinnamon rolls if said rolls will increase her bottom line! Unfortunately these cinnamon rolls are so good they are sure to increase your waistline as well, hence the name 'Coronaries in a basket cinnamon rolls!' They are also so quick and easy to make you are sure to want to make them all the time once you try them!

Makes 18 Cinnamon Rolls

Ingredients:

- 1 frozen bread dough loaf
- ½ stuck of unsalted butter
- 1 cup brown sugar
- 1 teaspoon of cinnamon

- ½ cup heavy whipping cream
- 1 cup of powdered sugar
- ½ cup of half and half
- ½ teaspoon vanilla extract

1. First thaw the bread dough for a whole day or overnight in a well oiled large bowl covered with a plate or saran wrap. After it's thawed and risen, roll it out into a ¼ inch wide large piece on a well floured surface.

2. Brush melted butter on the bread dough and then layer the brown sugar and then cinnamon on top of the butter. Roll the whole piece up into a pinwheel shape. Now cut the piece into about 18 slices about an inch and half wide with a wet knife.

3. Use shortening to grease 2 8 or 9 inch cake pans and place 9 rolls in each pan. Preheat an oven to 350 degrees while you let the rolls rise in the cake pans for about an hour. Pour the heavy whipping cream over the rolls right before baking.

4. Bake the rolls at 350 for 20 minutes. While the rolls are baking, use a electric mixer to mix the powdered sugar, milk and vanilla extract and then pour it over the rolls.

Georgie's Chocolate Banana Pancakes

Whenever Georgie's brother Jeff comes to visit the ranch, she is naturally overjoyed, so she made these delicious Chocolate Banana Pancakes to celebrate one of his visits. These delicious banana flavored pancakes are a tasty alternative to traditional plain pancakes, and are especially good when you have run out of maple syrup-because you can eat them covered with peanut butter instead. We used Canadian flour (which is self rising flour and gives the pancakes a more light and fluffy taste), in this recipe like we imagined Georgie would have, but if you can't find Canadian flour, you can try any other self rising flour like King Arthur's as a great substitute.

Though Jeff never ended up trying Georgie's pancakes, he didn't know what he missed, and you won't either unless you try these sweet fluffy flavorful pancakes!

Makes 8 pancakes

Ingredients:

- 1 cup Canadian or King Arthur's self rising flour
- 1 teaspoon white sugar
- 2 teaspoons baking powder
- Punch of salt
- 1 egg
- ½ cup milk

- 2 tablespoons of applesauce
- 1 cup bananas, mashed
- ½ cup of chocolate chips
- ½ teaspoon vanilla extract
- Optional toppings: peanut butter, powdered sugar

1. Combine all the dry ingredients in one mixing bowl: flour, sugar, baking powder and salt. Mix all the wet ingredients: the egg, milk, applesauce, mashed banana, and vanilla extract in another bowl. Then mix both together gently until just all the ingredients are mixed.

2. Pour ¼ cup of batter into a well oiled frying pan over low to medium heat. Since the pancakes have banana and chocolate in them they will be fairly darker than regular pancakes. Serve with peanut butter or powdered sugar on top or both! if so inclined.

Dude Ranch Low Cal Cowboy Special

Though the exact elements of this dish might be a little foggy, one thing we do know is that it definitely entailed bacon. This is because the Dude Ranch Cowboy Special was featured in an episode where Cassandra was supposed to serve it to a guest at the dude ranch who was well, uh to say tactfully a bit big boned, and because of his big boneness he was not allowed to go on a trail ride on any of the dude ranch horses. The guest is quite miffed that he will not be allowed to ride one of the horses. So Cassandra rather untactfully suggests that he might want to replace the bacon in the Cowboy Special with fruit as a lower calorie, lower in fat substitute. The guest was quite miffed with this suggestion as well. In Cassandra's defense she was merely looking out for the guest's health, and we are looking out for your health here as well. So we are presenting this recipe as a low cal yet tasty breakfast option as well-whether you are big boned or not!

Serves 1

Ingredients:

- 1 cup of nonfat cottage cheese
- ½ cantaloupe sliced
- ½ orange sliced
- 1 handful of raspberries
- 1 teaspoon of sugar
- Sprig of mint

1. Mix the cottage cheese with the sugar and arrange decoratively on a breakfast plate.

2. Place slices of cantaloupe and orange next to the cottage cheese. Sprinkle the cottage cheese with raspberries and a sprig of mint.

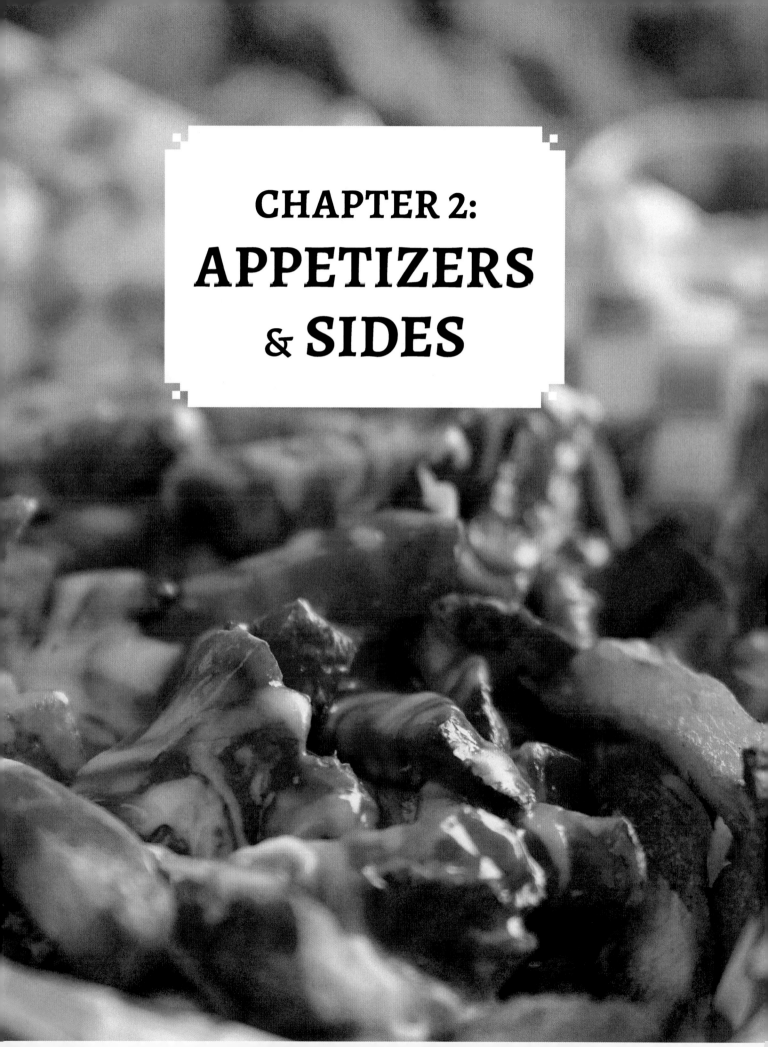

CHAPTER 2:
APPETIZERS & SIDES

Mrs. Bell's Prize Winning Adult Strawberry Jam

It's obvious that Lou isn't thrilled when Grandpa Jack suggests she spend 'all day' canning strawberry jam with Mrs. Bell, but by the end of the day she realizes it was a great business idea and extremely tasty as well! We called this Adult Strawberry Jam because it has a splash of liquor in it, but not to fear, all the alcohol evaporates out during the jam making process making it safe for children to consume as well. Of course, you can always leave the 'secret ingredient' in Mrs. Bell's jam out as well, but it just won't be the same, as Grandpa Jack attests to when the Heartland women make a batch without Mrs. Bell's 'secret ingredient'.

Ingredients:

- 1 pound of strawberries
- 1 cup of honey
- 1 tablespoon of lemon juice
- Secret ingredient: 1 ounce of dark rum

1. Cut stems off the strawberries and wash them carefully. Place all ingredients in a very large pot and let sit for about 15 to 30 minutes for all the flavors to meld together.

2. Then heat the mixture over medium high heat and cook for about 20 to 30 minutes.

3. Skim any foam off the top and throw it away. You will know when it's done because the mixture will start to get a jelly-like consistency. If you have a candy thermometer the temperature should read about 220 degrees F/ degrees C.

4. Once the mixture is thickening add the rum and cook for about 3 more minutes, then remove the pan from heat. If you plan to keep this jam around for a while like Mrs. Bell and Lou did use sterilized jars and canning procedures to store the extra jam.

Maggie's Institutional Poutine French Fries

As if being Mallory's first solid food isn't enough, Maggie's poutine french fries are your classic Canadian french fries. That is, thick potato slices fried and topped with creamy cheese curds, salty Ritz cracker crumbs and slathered in a savory gravy. These fries can be an accompaniment to such Maggie's classics such as the Maggie's Chicken Club or if Tim is ever able to convince Lou to put them on the menu, an accompaniment to his Time for Tim Jerk(y) chicken wings. Then again, with all the tasty toppings on these fries, they could be a meal in themselves!

Ingredients:

- 1 pound or 4 large Russet Potatoes
- 2 cups of peanut oil or any vegetable oil

- 1 teaspoon of salt

Gravy:

- 4 Tablespoons of butter
- 6 Tablespoons of flour
- 2 cups of beef stock
- 1 teaspoon of black pepper

- Cheese Curds: Just buy Cheese Curds (available at most grocery stores)
- Ritz Crackers: Just buy Ritz Crackers (available at most grocery stores), crumbled

1. Peel and cut potatoes into french fry size shapes. Place the cut potatoes into ice water for five minutes.

2. Next spread the potato sticks on paper towels or regular towels until they are bone dry. Heat the oil on medium high heat in a thick large pot, and drop in your potato sticks when the oil starts to slightly bubble. When the potatoes are only very slightly browned remove and place on paper towels with a large slotted spoon. Sprinkle it with salt.

3. For the gravy, melt butter over medium heat in a frying pan, once the butter is fully melted add flour and stir until it becomes light brown or what is traditionally called a Roux. Then add the beef stock abd continue to cook for 3 more minutes. Lastly add the black pepper.

4. To assemble Maggie's Institutional Poutine French Fries layer the fries at the bottom, next add the cheese curds, next pour the gravy over and top with the crumbled Ritz crackers. Voila!

Scott's Traditional Canadian Bannock

Though it wasn't really explained what the side dishes are for Scott's Prairie Oyster Stew it seems that a traditional Canadian bread called Bannock would be a nice accompaniment. Bannock is a flattish, round type of bread, similar to the American fried dough. It was originally a native food and is often included by First Nation bakers in their stock recipes. The biggest difference between Bannock and fried dough is that Bannock is both fried, and then baked, not just fried like fried dough, but if you want to make it a healthier version like we did here, you can just bake it.

Makes 6-8 Bannock

Ingredients:

- 2 cups flour
- 2 teaspoons baking powder
- 2 cups water (warm)
- ¼ cup butter
- 1 teaspoon salt

- 1 teaspoon sugar
- 2 Tablespoons butter
- Optional toppings: sunflower seeds, raisins and/or powdered sugar

1. Preheat your oven to 375 degrees F. Mix together the dry ingredients and then cut the butter into very small pieces (about ½ inch squares) and then put in the butter and water.

2. Knead the dough for about 1 minute. Now either using cooking spray or an oiled pan sprinkled with flour, place the dough in a loaf pan or cookie sheet and bake for 20 minutes until lightly golden brownƒ on the top.

Grandma Lyndy's Southern Biscuits

Years before Jackson Bartlett met Lyndy Payne; her father's sister, Aunt Mae, met an American and married him. They settled in North Carolina. Aunt Mae came home to Alberta one summer for a visit. She taught young Lyndy how to make Southern Biscuits from the mountains of North Carolina. Months later, Lyndy entered Aunt May's biscuit recipe in the Calgary Stampede's Cowgirl Cook-Off. She won first prize in the bread & biscuits category. A rodeo cowboy would be hard pressed to find a flakier & more flavorful biscuit, anywhere on the prairies of Alberta.

Makes 12 Biscuits

Ingredients:

- 2 cups all purpose flour
- 3 teaspoons baking powder
- 3/4 teaspoon baking soda
- 1/2 teaspoon salt

- 6 Tablespoons butter, cold
- 1 cup buttermilk, cold (full fat; avoid low fat)

1. Preheat the oven to 450 degrees F. Combine flour, baking powder, baking soda, and salt in a large bowl. Cover bowl with plastic wrap & place in freezer for 1 to 2 hours. Cut cold butter into flour with a pastry blender, until butter particles are pea sized. Add buttermilk & mix until just combined, being careful not to overwork dough.

2. Place dough onto a floured surface & roll out into a rectangle, then fold over. Repeat 2 more times; rolling out dough and folding it over. Roll out final time & cut with biscuit cutter to about 1/2 inch thickness.

3. Place on an ungreased baking pan. Bake in a 450 degree F oven for 5 minutes, then lower to 425 degrees F, and bake an additional 10 to 15 minutes; until golden brown.

Lou's Banana Muffins with a Crunch

When Lou makes these muffins it's for people who are willing to support her bid to buy Maggie's and keep it the downhome traditional Canadian diner. These banana muffins with a crunch define Lou in a way. That is, they embody her personality: sweet, but with a bite if you cross her! If you'd rather make these muffins in the form of a cake, just add 1 cup less of the mashed bananas and add an additional ¼ cup of brown sugar.

Makes 12 muffins or one 8 by 8 inch cakes

Ingredients:

- ⅓ cup brown sugar
- ¾ cup rolled oats
- 2 Tablespoons of butter, mostly melted
- ¼ cup of chopped walnuts
- ½ cup of oil
- 2 cups of bananas, mashed

- 2 eggs
- 1 teaspoon of vanilla extract
- 1¾ cup flour
- 1 teaspoon of baking soda
- 1 teaspoon of salt

1. Preheat the oven to 350 degrees F/175 degrees C. Either grease or use cupcake liners for a regular size muffin pan.

2. In a large mixing bowl, first mix all the dry ingredients: flour, baking soda and salt ,then mix together the oil, bananas and eggs with the dry mixture. Stir in the walnuts and pour by tablespoon into the muffin pan.

3. Next make a crunch topping by mixing the rolled oats, butter, and brown sugar. Sprinkle each little muffin with some of the crunch topping mix.

4. Bake the muffins for 25 to 30 minutes or until the muffins start to puff up and the edges are turning golden brown.

Georgie's Family Friendly Jam

When Georgie is doing her grade 5 science project Lou and Peter try to take over the project from her, making fancy paper mache volcanoes and batteries using a potato as a conductor. But sensible George has a better and tastier idea..a science project on kitchen chemistry. Her science project ends up being all about showing how acids and sugars can balance each other perfectly, just like the members of her adopted family. Though we never found out what grade George got on her science project, her idea of making strawberry jam gets an A in our book! You can also make this jam like Georgie does by using old mushy strawberries that are a bit beyond their prime, it's a great way to use up old mushy strawberries-besides tasting great too.

Makes 3-4 jars of Jam

Ingredients:

- 3 pints of strawberries
- 4 cups of sugar

- ⅓ cup of lemon juice

1. Wash, dry and then cut the stems off the strawberries. Slice the strawberries at least in half and in a large bowl toss them (gently) with the sugar. Cover the bowl and leave the strawberries to macerate (a fancy word for the flavors starting to meld together) for about 4 hours or even overnight.

2. Next, put the mixture into a large pan and bring to a boil over medium heat. Once boiling turn down and simmer for about 10 minutes stirring once in a while. There will be a lot of foam that is created by the reaction of the acid from the strawberries and the sugar. Try to skim off as much foam as you can. Use a metal spoon to skim.

3. Once the jam gets to a 'jam' thickness, take off of heat and let sit until cool. If you will be canning the jam, use proper canning techniques:

Time for Tim's Plank Roasted Bartlett Pears

It's no secret that Tim and Grandpa jac don't always get along. This often stems from Tim's constant needling and roasting of Grandpa Jack, so we thought roasted Bartlett pears might be in order. This dish would also serve as a great accompaniment to Tim's Planked Salmon (recipe on page 77) Though we don't officially know what Tim made as an accompaniment to his Plank Roasted Salmon, you might as well use the grill to make another planked dish while you're at it. You can even use the same plank twice, though we recommend you make the pears first and not the salmon because the fish smell might not come out of the plank after you use it to make salmon.

Serves 4

Ingredients:

- 1 cedar plank
- 2 large Bartlett pears (no relation to Jack Bartlett that we know of, but maybe that would be a great storyline hint hint writers of Heartland!)
- 2 Tablespoons Balsamic vinegar
- 2 Tablespoons of Amber honey (again no relation)
- ½ cup crumbled blue cheese
- 4 thyme sprigs

1. Soak the cedar plank for one hour in water. Meanwhile, turn your grill to medium high heat. Next, cut each Bartlett pear in half. And then remove the seeds from each half and make a little hole in each pear half and place an equal amount of the blue cheese in each pear half.

2. Now brush the vinegar over each half and then brush the honey over the vinegar. Put the water soaked plank into the grill and let heat up for about 5 minutes. Place the pear halves on the cedar plank and cover the grill.

3. Cook the pears until the edges of the pear halves start to turn brown, about 10 minutes. Drizzle any remaining honey over the top of the pears and garnish with the thyme sprigs.

CHAPTER 3:
MAIN DISHES

Maggie's Vegetarian Chili

One of the most iconic dishes from Maggie's Diner is the vegetarian chili. Almost every member of the Heartland family has talked about the Vegetarian Chili at some point on the show. Since Heartland takes place in 'cattle country' it's ironic that the most famous chili at Maggie's would be a vegetarian version of the comfort food favorite. Yet even picky cattle ranching, meat and potato eaters like Tim and Jack love it. You can make this insanely good vegetarian chili just with beans as the base, or add veggie grounds to give it more of a meaty texture and flavor.

Serves 4

Ingredients:

- ¼ cup of olive oil
- 1 cup onions, finely chopped
- ⅓ carrots, shredded or finely chopped
- 3 cloves garlic, finely chopped
- 1 cup green pepper, chopped
- 1 Tablespoon chili powder
- 1 cup mushrooms, chopped
- 1 large tomato, chopped
- 3 cups of V-8

- 1 can kidney beans (18 ounces)
- 1 can of corn (8 ounces)
- 1 Tablespoon ground cumin
- 2 teaspoons dried oregano
- 2 teaspoons dried basil
- ½ teaspoon salt
- ½ teaspoon black pepper
- 4 sprigs of cilantro for garnish

1. Heat the olive oil in a frying pan and cook the onions and carrots until soft over medium high heat, next add the garlic and cook for a minute or two mire. Add the green peppers, chili powder and cumin next and cook for five more minutes.

2. Next, stir in the mushrooms and cook everything for five more minutes. Stir in the beans, v8, tomatoes and corn. Lastly, garnish with oregano, basil, salt and pepper. Cover and simmer for 20 minutes, stirring occasionally.

Maggie's All Canadian Chicken Club

When Maggie's Diner changes hands from Maggie to Lou, one thing Lou is sure she wants for Maggie's is to keep it an authentic Canadian diner-even when her 'silent partner' and dad Tim wants to take it in another direction. After all, Maggie's was used as a stage post in the early 1900s according to Mallory, so we're betting this Canadian staple was one of the original items on the menu.

Ingredients:

- 2 4 oz chicken breasts
- 4 slices of white bread
- 2 slices of cheddar cheese
- 4 slices of bacon
- 2 burger rolls
- 3 cloves of garlic, crushed
- ½ cup of onion, finely chopped
- 1 tsp dijon mustard

- ½ cup ketchup
- ¼ cup maple syrup
- 2 tablespoons lemon juice
- 1 tablespoon Worcestershire sauce
- Pinch of black pepper
- pinch of cumin powder
- Optional toppings: lettuce, tomato slices, bell pepper slices

1. Pound the chicken breasts until they are ¼ inch thick. Cook bacon in a lightly oiled frying pan while doing this. Remove the bacon and cook the chicken breasts on medium high heat in the same pan until there is no pink in the middle, about 10 minutes.

2. While the chicken is cooking, mix together the onion, garlic, ketchup, mustard, maple syrup and Worcestershire sauce. Toast the bread in a toaster or at 350 in an oven on a baking sheet for 5 minutes.

3. Next assemble the sandwiches layering a slice of toasted bread, then lettuce, tomato slices, bell pepper slices, a piece of chicken, cheese then another slice of bread, a piece of bacon, a slice of cheese and sauce with another slice of bread on top.

Lou's Mostly Microwaved Shepherd's Pie

When Lou first comes back to the Heartland ranch from New York City, the last thing she seems to want to do is cook. After all, she is a high powered investment banker working for a Wall Street firm so cooking dinner for the Heartland family is low on her priority list. Maybe to save time though, she does quickly become well acquainted with the microwave though. Though the food she cooks using the microwave, including this dish, doesn't always get a warm reception from the rest of the Heartland family we feel we have tweaked it enough so you will enjoy its savory goodness while also enjoying the convenience of using the microwave to do most of the cooking!

Serves 6

Ingredients:

- 4 cups of potato flakes or 4 large potatoes
- 4 cups of hot water
- ½ cup of cheddar cheese
- 1 bag of frozen peas (8 oz)
- 1 can of mushrooms (8 oz)
- 1 bag of frozen corn (8 oz)
- 1 pound of ground beef or 1 pound of vege grounds (like Morningstar vege grounds)

- 1 teaspoon of worcestershire sauce
- ¼ cup of red wine
- 3 tablespoons of butter
- ¼ cup of olive oil
- 2 teaspoons of fresh or dried rosemary
- 2 egg whites

1. Warm the frozen corn in the microwave until warm, about 5 minutes. Mix the potato flakes and the hot water until mashed potato consistency, add the butter and the egg whites and stir. You can also use regular potatoes which you nuke in the microwave until soft, peel and add the butter and egg white.

2. Next, fry the ground beef or vege grounds in a frying pan with half the olive oil until mostly not pink. Add the worcestershire sauce and the red wine to the meat. In another pan put the rest of the olive oil and cook the carrots and mushrooms with the red wine until the red wine is almost gone, add the corn and stir.

3. Now, using a large casserole baking dish, layer the meat on the bottom of the dish, next layer the vegetables (corn, mushroom and carrot mixture) and lastly put the potatoes on the top. Cook in the microwave for 5 minutes. If you want the top of the potatoes to be crispy, put the pan in the oven at 400 for 5 minutes.

Janice's Jerky Chicken & Rice

Ask any Heartland fan and they will tell you that Janice is one of the most unpopular of Tim's girlfriends. She irritates everyone, even Amy who is always patient with everyone. When Janice is invited to dinner at the Heartland ranch, she brings her own food, she annoys Lou as this is the same night when Lou makes her famous Dishes of Dubai. Though Janice's simple chicken and rice dish is 'a hit' with the rest of the Heartland family, Janice herself most certainly isn't.

Serves 8

Ingredients:

To Make the Chicken:

- 4 chicken breasts, cut into 1 inch wide strips
- PAM 100% Fat-Free original Canola Oil cooking spray
- 1 teaspoon sugar
- 1 teaspoon soy sauce

- 1 teaspoon honey
- 1 teaspoon cumin
- ½ teaspoon garlic powder
- ¼ cup of lime juice

To Make the Rice:

- 4 cups of organic brown rice
- 6 cups of water

- 1 teaspoon of salt

1. First make a marinade for the chicken out of the sugar, soy sauce, honey, cumin, garlic powder and lime juice. Place the chicken breasts into a plastic bag or dish and soakin the marinade for about an hour.

2. Then drain the marinade and place the chicken on a baking sheet that has been sprayed with a little PAM cooking spray. If you have a rice cooker, cook the rice in it, otherwise boil the water in a large pot with the salt and then add the rice, cook for about 20 minutes covered, then uncover it and cook for about 10 more minutes. Fluff with fork.

Lou's Semi-Homemade Cordon Bleu

When Lou tries her hand at making this popular and scrumptious French dish, she is still in transition between her life at Heartland Ranch and her fast paced cosmopolitan life in New York City. So it's no surprise that her attempt at a Cordon Bleu probably includes ingredients that wouldn't be used by a five star chef or someone who takes their time in the kitchen. So though this dish doesn't appear to be a big hit with the Heartland family, we're fairly certain this version of Lou's Semi-Homemade Cordon Bleu has been tweaked enough to be a big hit with your family. And for all the busy cooks out there, we still used some store bought ingredients too...

Ingredients:

- 6 slices of deli ham, already cooked
- 6 slices of deli swiss cheese
- 6 chicken breasts
- ¼ cup of honey dijon mustard
- 1 cup italian bread crumbs
- ½ cup grated Parmesan cheese

- 4 tablespoons of mayonnaise
- Sprinkle of pepper, paprika and salt
- 2 Tablespoons of butter
- 1 tablespoon of flour
- 1 cup of milk or light cream
- ¼ cup of white wine

1. Pound the chicken to as flat as possible with a mallet. Place a ham slice on top of each chicken piece, and then a swiss cheese slice and smother with mustard. Place each piece side by side in an oven safe casserole pan and then spread mayonnaise on top of the chicken and sprinkle the parmesan cheese and breadcrumbs on top of that as well as the dry spices: salt, pepper and paprika.

2. Cover the casserole pan with aluminum foil and back for 20 minutes or until the chicken isn't pink and breadcrumbs look crusty. Meanwhile in a saucepan make a sauce by warming the butter and then when the butter starts to bubble up add flour and mix vigorously until the flour starts to lightly brown, then quickly add the milk or cream and wait a few minutes for the sauce to thicken. Add the wine last and serve the sauce on the side with the chicken.

Lisa's Fancy Turkey & Swiss Sandwiches

Lisa Stillman is as fancy as they get. She was married to millionaire and purported richest man in Hudson and racehorse owner Dan Hartfield at one point in her life, and she owns a large grand horse breeding operation where she breeds the finest quality, world class horses. The fact that she falls for Jack Bartlett who might seem a bit rough around the edges for Lisa might be a surprise to a few. But we think it's Lisa's knack for seeing Jack as a diamond in the rough that makes their relationship work. Another thing that makes their relationship work could be the fact that Lisa tries hard to make Jack feel comfortable, by serving him familiar comfort food like Turkey and Swiss sandwiches, while staying true to her own heritage and nature by giving them an elevated and delicious twist.

Serves 2

Ingredients:

- 4 slices of Brioche bread
- 2 Tablespoons of horseradish sauce
- 2 Tablespoons of Vegenaise mayonnaise or regular mayonnaise
- 6 slices of black pepper turkey breast, thinly sliced

- 6 slices of Baby Swiss cheese, thinly sliced
- 4 slices of red Vidalia onion
- 4 slices of bacon
- 4 crisp slices of lettuce

1. Fry the bacon in a small frying pan until crisp. Place the bacon slices on a paper towel to get out a lot of the bacon grease. Slice a Vidalia onion. Mix the horseradish sauce with mayonnaise.

2. Assemble the sandwiches by placing a piece of bread on a piece of wax paper or aluminum foil. Next, add the cheese, then turkey, then bacon, then onion and lettuce on top of that. Spread the horseradish/mayonnaise mixture on the other slice.

Grandpa Jack's Fishing Cabin Fish Fry

Whenever Grandpa Jack wants to get away to think or to do some spectacular fly fishing, he heads up to his rustic little fishing cabin nestled on a knoll near a perfect shallow part of the river for fly fishing. This cabin has a special significance for Jack in the sense that it's a place he went to with his first wife Lyndy when they were both young. The fishing cabin doesn't have much in terms of modern amenities like refrigerators and microwave ovens but that suits Jack just fine because then he can make one of his comfort classics with a fresh catch from the river like a fish fry. Trying to stay true to the rustic nature of the fishing cabin as well as Jack's penchant for simplicity as well, this fish fry is light on ingredients but heavy on flavor! Since Trout, walleye and pike are most likely the fish we think Grandpa Jack would have caught, we used trout in this recipe.

Serves 2

Ingredients:

- 4 trout filet slices
- ½ cup of barbecue sauce
- 1 lemon

- 4 Tablespoons of canola oil
- Sprinkle of black pepper, garlic powder and paprika

1. Place the oil in a large frying pan and heat over medium heat. Make about 6 cuts on one side of each filet so the fish will cook faster.

2. Place the trout filets directly into the pan and fry until crisp on both sides (about 5 minutes on each side).

3. Pour the barbecue sauce right on top of the filets and the dry spices: pepper, garlic powder and paprika and fry for a few more minutes. Serve with slices of lemon. If you have access to an outdoor grill like Grandpa Jack did you can cook the filets on a piece of aluminum foil on medium heat but substitute the oil for a mixture of 2 Tablespoons of butter and 2 Tablespoons of lemon juice. After about 10 minutes brush on the barbecue sauce and the dry spices and cook for another 3-5 minutes.

Lou's Dishes of Dubai Baba Ganoush

When Lou tasks Mallory with peeling the eggplant for the Middle Eastern dip she wants to make called Baba Ganoush. Mallory is hesitant about the whole plan, warning Lou that her whole plan might be a little too exotic for the Heartland family. Lou counters Mallory's complaint by saying that Baba Ganoush is delicious. She is certainly right about that! Just make sure to follow the directions very carefully on how to cook the eggplant, as eggplant can be bitter if not cooked correctly.

Serves 6

Ingredients:

- 1 eggplant, should be firm and medium in size
- 2 cloves of garlic
- 2 tablespoons of olive oil
- 2 tablespoons of lemon

- 2 tablespoons of tahini
- 2 sprigs of Italian flat leaved parsley
- Sprinkle of salt and pepper

1. Preheat the oven to broiling, about 425 degrees F/210 degrees C. To cook the eggplant: take an eggplant and make holes in it with a fork. Then wash it and sprinkle the skin with salt. Wrap the eggplant in aluminum foil and broil it until it feels soft, turning it every 10-15 minutes, it will take about 30-45 minutes to cook.

2. Next, remove the eggplant from the oven, unwrap the aluminum foil and let it sit until it's a bit cool. Then rinse the salt off the eggplant, and scoop the insides of the eggplant into a bowl or right into a food processor.

3. Add the lemon juice, tahini, garlic, salt and pepper to the eggplant and mash it by hand or in a food processor. Last mix in the olive oil. This dish is best if it's refrigerated for a few hours before serving.

Lou's Dishes of Dubai Basmati Rice Pilaf

Though a fruit tree orchard hasn't been shown to be a feature on the Heartland Ranch, we really feel that somewhere on all those 600 acres there's a beautiful little alcove of fruit trees, probably mostly apple trees, peach trees, and a few Bartlett pear trees. Any of these sweet fruits would make an excellent addition to a Middle Eastern pilaf which is part of Lou's special Middle Eastern dinner or as we like to call them: The Dishes of Dubai. If you don't have any fresh fruit to make this with, you can also use dried fruit of any sort, it's excellent like that as well.

Ingredients:

- 2 cups of Basmati Rice
- 3 cups of water
- 4 Tablespoons of Butter or olive oil
- 1 cup of onions, finely chopped
- 4 cloves of garlic, minced

Spices:

- 1 teaspoon of salt
- 1 teaspoon of cumin
- 1 teaspoon of turmeric
- Sprinkle of cinnamon

Toppings:

- ½ cup of fresh or dried fruit like apples, or dried apples, raisins, finely chopped
- ½ cup of sliced almonds toasted in butter or oil until lightly browned

1. Place the rice in a large bowl and cover it with water, then carefully pour out the water leaving just the rice in the bowl. You can make this dish faster and more conveniently if you use a rice cooker, but if you don't have a rice cooker, place the rice to the side for now.

2. Next, melt the butter or warm the oil over medium heat. Add the chopped onion and saute until very slightly brown, then add the garlic, and the cumin, turmeric and cinnamon until you can smell them all cooking, about 1 minute.

3. Add the rice and stir constantly for about a minute. Add the salt and water and bring the mixture to a boil. Reduce the heat to low now and cook for about 20 minutes. If you are using a rice cooker and the rice is already done, omit the water and use a little extra oil to just fry the rice slightly with the onion, spices and garlic mixture for less than a minute.

Lou's Dishes of Dubai Middle Eastern Meatball (Kofta) Curry

Kofta is a traditional Middle Eastern main dish that is so flavorful and fun. It's traditionally made with either lamb or beef as the staple protein. Because Heartland is a cattle ranch, we used beef as the main protein, but you can use lamb or make a vegetarian version of Kofta as well using one of the many vegetarian meatballs sold commercially such as Gardein's, MorningStar, and Beyond Meat brands. They all make very tasty and nutritious meat alternatives.

Ingredients:

- 1 bag of frozen beef meatballs, or vege meatballs
- 1 medium size onion, chopped
- 2 large tomatoes, chopped
- 1 green hot pepper, take out the seeds if you don't want your tongue to burn!
- 2 teaspoon ground cumin
- ½ teaspoon of cinnamon
- 5 garlic cloves, chopped

- ½ inch piece of ginger, finely chopped or crushed
- 3 tablespoons of plain yogurt
- 1 teaspoon coriander powder
- ½ teaspoon turmeric powder
- 1 teaspoon of salt
- 2 cups of water
- ½ teaspoon of garam masala
- 2 tablespoon of dried cilantro or a handful of fresh cilantro leaves

Instructions

1. Use a large frying pan or pot, fry the onions with all the dried spices on medium high heat for 5 minutes. Then add the garlic and ginger and saute for another 2 minutes before adding the tomatoes, hot pepper and yogurt.

2. Saute for an additional 5 minutes. Next add the water and the frozen meatballs and bring the whole mixture to a boil, then reduce the heat and cook everything at a simmer for 30 minutes.

Grandpa Jack's Beef Stew in a Jar

Grandpa Jack's knack for putting together simple food is something any cook would love to emulate. This dish, Beef Stew in a Jar, was one of his favorites. Jack is a practical cook, so using a jar to measure his spices makes good practical sense. The only bad thing about using a jar to measure your spices is if you lose your jar, you have no idea how much of each seasoning and ingredient to put in the stew. So you can make this recipe in a jar if you want to..but don't worry we gave you more traditional measurements as well.

Serves 6

Ingredients:

- 2 Tablespoons of Olive Oil
- 2 medium yellow onions, coarsely chopped
- 1 bag of baby carrots or 4 regular carrots cut into large chunks
- 1 pound of small sized Yukon Gold potatoes
- 5 cloves of garlic, coarsely chopped

- 2 pounds of Beef Sirloin tips cut into about 1 inch pieces, (or for Vegetarians 1 inch chunks of Seitan)
- 2 cups of Beef Broth
- 2 Tablespoons of Worcestershire Sauce
- 2 cups of water

Jar Ingredients (dry ingredients):

- 2 teaspoons of Salt
- 1 teaspoon of Thyme
- 1 teaspoon of Basil

- 1 teaspoon of black pepper
- 1 bay leaf
- ½ cup of flour

1. Heat a large pot like a Dutch oven with the olive oil on medium heat. Saute the onions for a few minutes then add the carrots and cook together for about 5 minutes.

2. Then add the potatoes and garlic and also add a little more oil if needed. Cook for another 10 minutes.

3. Place the beef tips in the jar and shake it altogether. Place the meat in a frying pan with a bit of oil and sear the meat on both sides for a minute or two. Throw the meat, and the remaining flour and spices mixture into the pot holding the vegetables and stir. Now pour in the beef broth and water.

4. Pour the Worcestershire sauce into the frying pan to scrape off any meat bits and pour that ito the pot as well. Add some additional salt and pepper and cover and cook the stew for about 20 more minutes.

Grandpa Jack's Alberta Butter Burger

Everyone knows that Grandpa Jack is no novice at grilling. He especially likes to make traditional good ole Canadian food like these Butter Burgers. Now Grandpa Jack might like grilling but that doesn't mean he's interested in fussing around with food and he's certainly not interested in creating anything someone might call fine dining. He leaves that to Lisa! Instead, he enjoys making simple manly filling foods on his barbeque grill. And as he's told Tim, he's been grilling for fifty years so he's pretty good at it, and this butter burger is no exception. The soft creamy butter melds perfectly with the sweet onions and tart cheddar cheese to make the best burger west of Saskatchewan.

Serves 6

Ingredients:

- 6 Tablespoons of salted butter, softened
- 1 medium size Vidalia or sweet onion, roughly chopped
- 1 Tablespoon of water
- 1 pound of ground beef

- 3 Tablespoons of Canola oil
- 6 Hamburger buns
- 6 slices of Cheddar Cheese
- Pinch of black pepper

1. Lightly salt and pepper the ground beef and shape into patties about ½ an inch thick. Next, place the chopped onions in a frying pan with the canola oil and water and cook until the onions start to get soft.

2. Next, turn the grill on hugh and heat until hot, about 10 minutes for most grills. After cleaning and oiling the cooking grate, place the patties on the grill and cook until well done on one side, flip and cook until mostly done, then add the cheese until its mostly melted.

3. Place a tablespoon of salted butter on each bun and then the cheese topped patty on top of that. Spread a little bit of cooked onions on the patty and cover with the other bun.

Grandpa Jack's Montreal Style Steak

When Mitch Cutty, Jack's ranch hand and Lou's on again/off again boyfriend and Jack have a disagreement on the best way to make a steak, they enter into a little competition. Jack enters his old fashioned steak which is just a steak seasoned with a little salt and Montreal seasoning, and Mitch enters his steak cooked in a water bath (recipe on page 79). Though Mitch ends up winning the steak competition for his steaks cooked in the water bath, we have a feeling that if Jack would have served his simple old fashioned steak with his steak compound butter and seasoned his steak with Montreal steak seasoning, he would have easily won. Grandpa Jack being the wise generous Good ole Canadian guy that he is, maybe he let Mitch win?

Serves 2

Ingredients:

- 2 Rib Eye steaks (½ pound or so each)
- Kosher salt

Montreal steak seasoning

- 2 Tablespoons of softened butter
- 1 Tablespoon onion, very finely chopped
- 1 clove of garlic, very finely chopped
- ½ Tablespoon chives, finely chopped

- ½ Tablespoon flat leaved Italian parsley, finely chopped
- Salt and pepper to taste, about ¼ teaspoon each

Instructions

1. Heat your grill to medium high or if cooking inside use a shallow frying pan with a little bit of oil on it. Season the steak with the Kosher salt and Montreal steak seasoning, Once the grill or pan is heated up cook the steak until desired doneness.

2. To make the compound butter for the steak place the butter with the onion, garlic, chives, salt and pepper into a bowl and mix it altogether until its a rich buttery paste consistency.

Marnie's Steamed Burgers on a Bun

Marnie runs a catering business and like any caterer we are sure she likes to create flavorful food with the least amount of prep time and fuss. But as a caterer you also want something that is a bit different from the norm and memorable. Steamed Cheeseburgers fit that bill. To steam the burgers you have to use a Duch over or other large stockpot with a metal strainer or steamer basket you can fit inside. Steamed Cheeseburgers are a great party food and easy to make in bulk, but whether you are making these for six or sixty you're sure to enjoy these soft flavorful burgers.

Serves 6

Ingredients:

- 1½ pounds of ground beef
- 2 teaspoons of soy sauce
- 1 teaspoon of onion powder
- 1 teaspoon of tomato paste
- Pinch of black pepper

- ½ cup shredded cheddar cheese
- 6 hamburger buns
- Optional toppings: lettuce, onion slices, tomato slices

1. Mix soy sauce, onion powder, tomato paste and black pepper into the ground beef. Next shape the beef into patties about 4 inches across and ½ inch thick and season with salt.

2. Place a steamer basket or a stainless steel colander into a large stock pot or Dutch oven. Place the patties inside and cook until burgers are medium well done, about 7 to 8 minutes.

3. Take the patties out and place each on a burger bun, then top the burger patty with some of the sliced cheddar cheese.

4. Place burger bun tops on the burger patty and place each burger all assembled back into the steamer basket or colander in the Dutch oven. Let sit for about 30 seconds.

Lisa's Fancy Lobster Chili

With having a second home in the south of France and a membership to Hudson's exclusive polo club, it's obvious that Lisa is quite wealthy. With her old world wealth she has quite expensive taste and so we felt that when Lisa makes chili, it couldn't just be a recipe with some beans and ground beef mixed in, it needed to be fancy. This lobster chili has the consistency of a chili, the spice of a chili with a more fancy decadent bent to it. If you don't want to spend half your grocery money on expensive lobster, you can use crab instead.

Serves 6

Ingredients:

- 2 lbs of lobster meat
- 1 16 ounce bag of frozen corn
- 8 cups of water
- 8 Poblano peppers
- 4 zucchini, chopped

- 1 medium onion, chopped
- 1 teaspoon dried Oregano
- Pinch of salt
- Pinch of black pepper

Instructions

1. In a large pot, fry the onion until lightly browned over medium high heat. Next, add the zucchini and cook until tender, then add the lobster meat and the poblano peppers and cook for about 5 more minutes.

2. Turn the heat up to high, add the water and corn and bring everything to a boil, then turn down the heat and cook for about 20 minutes.

3. Lastly, add the oregano and the salt and pepper to taste.

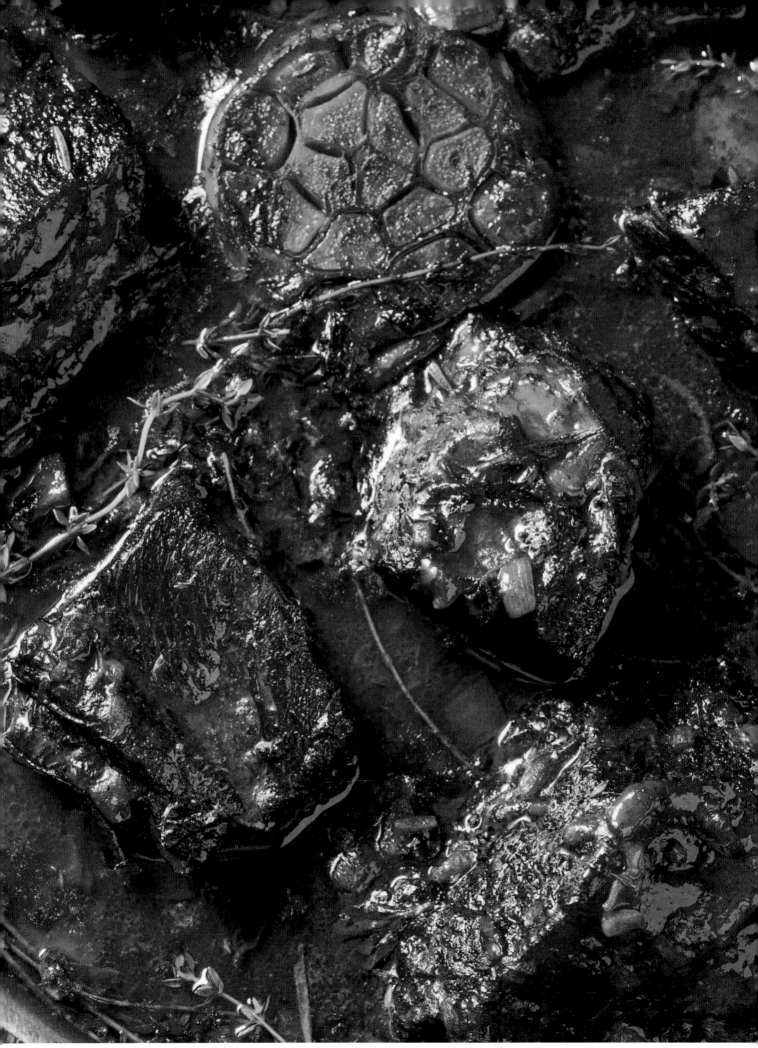

Lou's Elevated Short Rib Chili

Never to be outdone by Lisa, Lou also enjoys the finer things in life-though maybe not on the same level as Lisa. Regardless, here's Lou's recipe for chili which is a modern and slightly elevated take on a basic chili. Having been raised in cattle country, Lou's recipe is sure to be beef heavy, but using short ribs as her cut of meat makes this recipe a real standout. Another great thing about it, is it is perfect for busy moms like Lou because it is best made in a slow cooker-where you can 'set it and forget it'. So while Lou is busy with her multiple businesses, her messy love life and battling with everyone around her she can 'cook' this sure to be crowd pleaser with ease, and now so can you!

Ingredients:

- 4 pounds of bone in short ribs
- Pinch of salt
- Pinch of black pepper
- 2 Tablespoons ground cumin
- 1 Tablespoon ground coriander
- 4 Tablespoons chili powder
- 2 tablespoons sweet paprika
- 1 teaspoon of salt

- 1 Tablespoon of oregano
- 1 tablespoon sugar
- 1 Tablespoon olive oil
- 2 onions, chopped
- 2 canned chipotle chiles in Adobo sauce, chopped
- 1 28 ounce can of tomato sauce or 4 large chopped tomatoes

1. Season the short ribs with salt and pepper and then place them In a large skillet.

2. Next, brown the short ribs until the edges are slightly brown, then transfer the ribs to a large slow cooker. Using the same skillet, fry the onions until lightly browned, then add the cumin, coriander, chili powder and paprika, and cook for two more minutes. Pour this mixture into the slow cooker.

3. Add the tomato sauce or chopped tomatoes, sugar, canned chipotle chiles in Adobo sauce, salt and oregano to the slow cooker and cook everything on slow for about 8 hours (doesn't have to be exact).

Caleb's Trailer Fare: Beer Steak

Most of the time when we see Caleb at his trailer, he has a beer in one hand and grill tongs in the other. Since he loves grilling so much, mixing the two together just would make sense to him, so here's a simple recipe for Beer Steak. Since Caleb is from Okotoks we include a Canadian beer (Molson's Canadian) in this recipe. Just please don't use a light beer! Caleb is a cowboy after all, and cowboys aren't known for their light beer drinking. Caleb even grills in the middle of the frigid Alberta winters.. he's one crazy cowboy, yes he is!

Makes 2 Steaks

Ingredients:

- ½ pound Rib Eye steaks, 2 of them
- 1 bottle or can (12 ounces) Molson Canadian Fireside Lager Dark Beer or another Dark

1   Tablespoon of lemon pepper

- Beer of your choice
- 1 Tablespoon of salt
- 1 Tablespoon of lemon pepper

1. Place steaks in a large plastic bag or container. Make fork marks on the steaks and season with the salt and lemon pepper. Very slowly pour the beer on top of the steaks as to not lose any of the spices. Marinate for an hour or two.

2. Grill the steaks on high heat on an oiled grill until they are not too pink or done to your liking. Discord the rest of the marinade or continue to use it to keep the steaks moist.

Scott's Prairie Oyster Stew Cowboy Caviar Stew

When Lou's first guests arrive for the dude ranch, Scott is not nearly as excited as she is. Not because he doesn't want to support Lou in her new business venture, but because he is mistaken to be a Native Guide by her visitors instead of her boyfriend. Though Scott goes along with the ruse to help Lou, spending time with Lou's overnight visitors wasn't what he had in mind for that evening. However, Scott makes the best of it by playing along as a Native Guide and incorporates a distinctly Western delicacy into the main dish of the evening-prairie oysters.

Prairie Oysters are, (and there's really no easy way to put this) bull's testicles. Prairie Oysters are also called Cowboy Caviar since it's so distinctly western-and weird. For people that are squeamish to try Cowboy Caviar you can substitute short ribs or another tough cut of beef into this recipe, and if the thought of eating bull testicles turns you off from eating meat altogether, (and we really don't blame you), you can use Gardein Veggie Beef Tips in this recipe as a substitute as well.

Ingredients:

- 2 lbs of Prairie Oysters
- 1 cup flour
- ¼ cup olive oil
- 2 Tablespoons garlic, chopped
- 2 teaspoons of onions, sliced
- ½ cup Butter
- ½ bottle of red wine

- 1 large tomato, finely chopped
- 1 teaspoon chives, chopped if fresh or dried
- 1 teaspoon parsley, chopped if fresh or dried
- Pinch of salt
- Pinch of pepper

1. If you are crazy, we mean brave enough to try the bull testicles, first remove the touch outer skin with a knife. Then slice each 'oyster' into about ½ inch cubes. Season the oyster cubes with the flour and a little salt and pepper.

2. Next, heat oil in a frying pan and saute the onions for five minutes until lightly brown,m then add the garlic and the oyster cubes. Fry until everything is golden brown. Pour in the wine and chopped tomato. Simmer the mixture for about 30 minutes or until the oysters start to get a bit soft. Add the chives and parsley.

Lou's Dishes of Dubai: Tabbouleh

A traditional and delicious Middle eastern side dish, Lou makes Tabbouleh for the Heartland family when she first comes back home from Dubai. She is still in that denial stage and keeps going on and on about how much she loves being in Dubai and loves everything about it, even though it turns out none of that is true. Though Lou might not have liked Dubai very much, you're sure to like this dish. It's delicious and is so good for you. Not only that, if you have a vegetable and herb garden like they do at Heartland, you can use some of your delicious garden tomatoes, mint and parsley to make this dish even more healthy and delicious.

Serves 6

Ingredients:

- 1 cup Bulgur
- 2 cups of water
- 2 large bunches of flat leaf parsley, finely chopped (stems and all)
- 12-15 mint leaves, more finely chopped

- 1 cup of red onion like a Vidalia, finely chopped
- 1/2 cup of olive oil
- 1/4 cup of lemon juice
- 2 large tomatoes, chopped
- Salt and pepper to taste

1. Cook the bulgur in a dish with the water until it softens just slightly. It will take about 5 minutes.

2. Strain the bulgur and then mix all the ingredients together in a large casserole dish. Let stand for 30 minutes.

Lisa's Green Eyed Monster Five Alarm Venison Stew

Like most successful women, Lisa might seem to have a good amount of confidence, but when she feels like her relationship with her man is threatened-watch out! So when she comes home from her vacation home in France to find Val Stanton in the Heartland kitchen being friendly with Jack, she gets understandably ruffled about it. And when Jack unwittingly adds fuel to the fire by inviting Val to stay for dinner, this makes Lisa really steamed. That is why we imagine this venison stew to be quite spicy, just like the sparks that fly back and forth between these two female titans.

Serves 6

Ingredients:

- 1 pound of venison meat (cut in 2 inch cubes like thigh meat)

- 3 potatoes peeled and chopped into 1 inch pieces

- 1 small bag of baby carrots (16 ounces)

- 1 small container of mushrooms (16 ounces)

- 1 onion, chopped

- 4 cloves of garlic, chopped

- 2 cups of V8 or tomato sauce

- 1 cup red wine or marsala wine

- Dry spices: salt, pepper, paprika, red pepper flakes

Instructions:

1. Microwave the potatoes for 5 minutes and then peel and cut them into 1 inch pieces.

2. Next place the venison in a frying pan and brown it for about 5 minutes over medium high heat. Transfer the potatoes and venison to the crock pot.

3. Next, put the carrots, onion, garlic, tomato sauce (or V8), red wine and dry spices: salt, pepper, paprika and Italian red pepper flakes into the crock pot.

4. Cook on high for 4 hours or until carrots start to get soft, or on low for 7-8 hours.

Bison Burgers with Texas Corn Salad

Tim Fleming is a sort of annoying fellow on Heartland. Though his heart is often in the right place, he often says and does the wrong thing. Like when he wants to tear down Maggie's in order to turn it into a Bison Burger franchise. He doesn't seem to care that it really bothers his daughter Lou. The only thing he does right in the situation is expound that a bison burger franchise would do really well in Hudson, because well bison burgers he claimed were better than beef burgers which we agree with. It's pretty clear Tim is obsessed with Bison products and after eating this Grilled Bison Burger with Texas Corn Salad maybe you will be too. The Texas Corn Salad is a nod to the fact that Alberta is often called the Texas of the North.

Makes 6 Burgers

Ingredients:

- 1 pound of ground bison
- 6 pretzel rolls
- ½ cup of shredded parmesan cheese
- ½ stick of butter
- 6 ears of corn
- 3 Tablespoons of Vegannaise
- 1 garlic clove

- ½ cup lime juice
- ½ cup chopped scallions
- ½ cup feta cheese, crumbled
- ½ cup cilantro, chopped
- 1 Jalapeno, chopped
- Pinch of salt

Instructions

1. Preheat your grill to medium heat and after placing aluminum foil down, mix the ground bison with the parmesan cheese and shape into ½ inch patties. Brush each patty with butter and grill until desired doneness. Place each patty on a pretzel roll.

2. To make the Texas corn salad, grill the corn on medium heat on the grill and then cut off the corn with a knife into a large bowl. Add the mayo, garlic, lime juice, and mix with thecorn well. Top with the feta cheese, cilantro, jalapeno, pinch of salt and paprika.

Time for Tim's Salmon on a Plank

When Tim used the very expensive wine Jack was saving for Lisa to make this dish, Jack was furious. As usual, Tim had no consideration for others and only thought of himself as he poured the expensive wine over the salmon. In Tim's mind, it's always time for Tim! So instead of admitting his mistake, Tim tries to cover up his mistake with the fact that everyone thought the salmon was delicious so it was fine for him to use Jack's wine. However, you don't need to use very expensive wine to make this dish delicious. In fact, you can even use very cheap wine, so as usual Tim's excuses don't hold much water! Or wine in this case..

Serves 6

Ingredients:

- 1½ pounds of salmon filets, cut 1 inch thick
- 1½ cups Champagne vinaigrette
- 3 Tablespoons Dijon mustard
- ½ cup finely chopped mixed Italian herbs (like parsley, basil, oregano), fresh is best
- Pinch of salt

- Pinch of pepper
- Cedar wood grilling plank
- 2 cups of wine, any kind but red is preferable
- 2 cups of water

Instructions

1. Soak the cedar wood grilling plank in the wine and water for an hour, set aside. Meanwhile, in a large ziplock bag combine all the ingredients except the salt and pepper. Shake the bag gently to mix everything and let the mixture sit in the refrigerator to marinate for about 30 minutes.

2. Next, preheat a grill to medium high heat and place the cedar plank in it with the salmon placed on top of it on the grill. Cover the grill and cook for about 10-15 minutes.

Mitch's Steak in a Water Bath

For many people, the perfect steak is as elusive as Amy's heart in season 2.

You love your slab of meat, medium rare, but it returns to you rare or medium, raw or burnt. But now, for the aficionado of the New York strip steak, hope is as close as Mitch Cutty. His 'Sous Vide' or 'Steak in a Water Bath', is as welcome as Ty Borden in a bear fight!! The French perfected Sous Vide, & when translated means: 'Low temperature long time'. Mitch enjoys his steak with garlic butter mushrooms, fresh asparagus or Brussels Sprouts, mashed potatoes, or Mac & cheese. Set the mood with a nice Cabernet wine, and a Lemongrass or cherry blossom candle. Or, be a real cowboy & eat yours while sitting on a tree stump!!

Ingredients:

- 8 to 12 ounce New York Strip, Ribeye, T-Bone, or Porterhouse steak, at least 1 inch thick.

- 1 gallon Zip Lock bag

- 1 Tablespoon Butter

- 2 Tablespoon Olive oil

- Sous Vide cooker / immersion circulator machine

- Sous Vide container

- Cast iron skillet to sear steak

- Pinch of Kosher salt

- Pinch of black pepper

1. Fill the Sous Vide container with water per your machine's directions. Insert sous vide cooker. Using the chart, set to 5-10 degrees lower than the final desired internal temperature of meat.Rare 130 degrees F Medium rare 140 degrees F Medium 155 degrees F Well done 165 degrees.

2. When sous vide cooking is complete, seer the steak, which will raise the final internal temperature, 5 to 10 degrees F. Salt & pepper both sides of steak & let sit for 15 minutes. Place steak in a Ziplock bag with 1 Tablespoon butter. Seal bag well & immerse in sous vide machine.

3. Cook for 2 hours, or up to 4 hours. Extending cooking time will not change the doneness of steak. However, cooking for over 4 hours will degrade the meat's texture. Remove steak from bag, discard water & bag, & set steak on a plate to rest. Heat 2 Tablespoons olive oil, in a large cast iron skillet, or heavy frying pan, over high heat. Sear steak for 1 minute on each side. Set on a serving plate & let sit for 5 minutes before serving..

Lou's Sweet & Sour Tofu

Lou's sweet and sour tofu was almost like a metaphor for her on again/off again relationship with Mitch. It was both sweet...and sour. Like when Lou cooks up this vegan dish for Mitch's new girlfriend Maya. All the while Lou is still pining after Mitch herself and she ends up getting back together with Mitch again-at least temporarily. The key to this dish is making sure to squeeze every bit of water out of the tofu that you can. Think of an ex that you are still hung up on and angry with like maybe Lou did!

Serves 6

Ingredients:

- 1 package of extra firm tofu (8 ounces)
- ½ cup Canadian maple syrup
- ½ cup pineapple juice

- 1 Tablespoon of soy sauce
- 1 Tablespoon of sesame seeds
- 2 Tablespoons of honey dijon mustard

1. Take tofu out of the container and press water out like you are wringing out a sponge (or wringing your ex's neck whichever you prefer). Next place it between 2 paper towels to dry it further. Then cut into 1 inch square cubes.

2. Heat about 2 Tablespoons of oil in a frying pan and cook the tofu in the pan over medium high heat until the tofu starts to get browned on the edges.

3. Then add the maple syrup, pineapple juice, mustard and soy sauce and cook together for about 3 more minutes. Take off heat and garnish with sesame seeds.

Lou's Black Bean Quinoa Buddha Bowl

Lou's idea to make a Black Bean Buddha Bowl we believe stemmed partially from her hosting a horse yoga retreat at the Dude Ranch for Mitch's girlfriend Maya. Since Maya is a vegan, Lou is determined to make not just one excellent vegan dish but several-including this Black Bean Buddha Bowl. A Buddha Bowl is usually a complete meal in itself as it includes: whole grains, vegetables, protein, and an optional topping like dressing and nuts or herbs. So there was really no need for Lou to make additional vegan dishes, but of course this is Lou here, who thinks nothing of having several full time jobs while raising two daughters...overkill is her middle name. (Actually Louise is her middle name)! But you get what we mean...

Serves 6

Ingredients:

- 1 cup Quinoa or Basmati rice
- ½ bag of frozen corn (8 ounces)
- 1 can of back beans (8 ounces)
- ½ cup shaved carrots

- 1 handful of crisp lettuce
- ½ cup of diced tomatoes
- ¼ cup balsamic glaze
- ¼ cup lime juice

1. Place 1 cup of quinoa in 1 cup of water in a sauce pan and bring to a boil. Once it's boiling take the pan off the stove and let sit for five minutes. If you cant or dont want to eat quinoa you can make rice for the Buddha bowl instead. If you have a rice cooker that's perfect.

2. Place the cup of rice in the rice cooker with 2 cups of water and turn it on. If you don't have a rice cooker, place the cup of water in 2 cups of salted boiling water and cook at a boil for 20 minutes uncovered. Meanwhile, drain the beans and rinse them in water. Also, microwave the frozen corn for about 5 minutes until warm. Arrange the rice, corn, beas, carrots, lettuce and tomato in a large decorative serving bowl all stacked next to each other. Last drizzle with the balsamic glaze and lime juice.

Lou's Bright Purple Pesto Pasta

Another flavorful and extremely colorful addition to Lou's vegan madness meal was purple pesto pasta. This pasta gets its strangely bright purple color from beets and the Heartland family was noticeably taken aback by the sight of such strange food stuff on their table. That doesn't mean they turned their noses up at the dish. In true polite Canadian fashion, both Amy and Ty tried the purple colored pasta and seemed pleasantly surprised by its pleasing and delicate flavor. The earthy flavor of the beet pasta is perfectly paired with the tangy garlic and pine nut taste of the pesto.

Serves 6

Ingredients:

- 1 cup fresh basil leaves
- 4 cloves of garlic, finely chopped
- 4 tablespoons of pine nuts
- ½ cup grated Parmesan cheese

- ½ cup olive oil
- 3 beets
- 1 package of linguine pasta

1. First boil the beets for about 20 minutes until you can peel them easily and slice them into ½ inch pieces. Next boil the linguine in a bit of a stockpot of salted water.

2. While the linguine is cooking, use a food processor to mix the basil leaves, garlic, pine nuts, olive oil and parmesan cheese into a thick sauce like consistency.

3. After draining the linguine, mix the beets and pesto in with the pasta.

Maggie's Favorite Fried Chicken

Maggie's diner specializes in down home Canadian comfort food and their fried chicken recipe is no exception. This is a common goto for the Heartland family on days when no one has time to cook-which is a lot of days. For example, when Georgie is working at Maggie's Diner she is also going to school, doing trick riding, learning high level show jumping, so needless to say she is very busy. Her mother Lou is no less busy with owning not one but two businesses: the Heartland Dude Ranch and Maggie's Diner. Being able to grab some fried chicken from Maggie's must be a God send. Plus it's downright the best Fried Chicken you could ever have!

Ingredients:

- Cut up a 4 pound whole chicken into pieces, or purchase 4 pounds of your favorite chicken parts.
- 1 cup buttermilk
- 1 egg, beaten
- 2 cups all purpose flour
- 1/4 teaspoon sage

- 1/2 teaspoon garlic powder
- 1 teaspoon paprika
- 1/2 teaspoon salt
- 1/2 teaspoon black pepper
- 1/8 teaspoon dry mustard

1. In a resealable bag, combine flour, sage, garlic powder, paprika, salt, pepper & dry mustard. Seal bag & shake to combine ingredients. In a bowl, beat the egg, then gently whip in buttermilk. Thoroughly dip chicken in buttermilk, egg mixture, then add a few pieces at a time to the flour mixture. Seal bag, and shake to coat chicken well.

2. Arrange chicken on a cookie sheet, cover loosely with wax paper, and allow coating to dry slightly, until it reaches a paste-like consistency. Pour vegetable oil into a large skillet, to a 3/4 inch depth. A cast iron skillet will help keep oil temperature consistent. Add heat & bring oil up to 350 degrees. Add 3 or 4 pieces of breaded chicken at a time into oil, and cook for 14-15 minutes, turning once, halfway through. Keep oil at, or close to 350 degrees during the entire cooking process. Chicken is done when the internal cooking temperature reaches 165 degrees, on a meat thermometer. Remove from oil & place on paper towels.Let rest 10-15 minutes before serving.

Katie Cooking for a Cause: Ketchup Lasagna

Katie first makes this dish when she is 13 years old and starting to become a teenager and her own person. So it's not surprising that she would want to show her family that she can cook dinner. When Lisa says she can, she is determined to find a way to do it, and comes up with her own spin on Lisa's classic lasagna with her own version made with ingenuity, spunk and whatever was left over in the Heartland pantry! Since there was no tomato sauce in the Heartland pantry that day, Katie ingeniously decides to use ketchup instead. We tweaked Katie's recipe a bit and used both ketchup and tomato sauce, because ketchup is much sweeter than tomato sauce. So if your taste buds are more sophisticated than a four year old's then without loads of ketchup it will taste a lot better as well!

Ingredients:

- 2 Tablespoons of olive oil
- 1 cup of ricotta cheese
- 4 Tablespoons of Italian flat leaf parsley, chopped
- 1 pound of ground beef
- 1 cup onion, chopped
- 4 cloves garlic, chopped
- 1 teaspoon dried Italian seasoning
- ½ teaspoon salt

- ½ teaspoon black pepper
- ⅓ cup water
- 4 fresh tomatoes, chopped
- ½ cup of ketchup
- 1 ½ cans of tomato sauce
- 9 dry lasagna noodles
- 3 cups of shredded mozzarella cheese

1. Preheat the oven to 350 F. Use either cooking spay or olive oil to grease a 9 by 13 cake pan or glass baking dish. Heat a frying pan using medium heat, and add the ground beef and onion. Once the beef isn't pink anymore add the garlic, salt, black pepper and Italian seasoning. Add the water, tomatoes, tomato sauce and ketchup to the meat and cook all of it for about 5 more minutes. Mix the ricotta cheese with the parsley and a little water (2 tablespoons) and a ½ cup of mozzarella cheese.

2. Put a little bit of the meat and tomato sauce mixture, about ½ a cup on the bottom of the baking dish and spread it around. Next, lay down 3 lasagna noodles and cover them with 1 cup more of the meat and tomato sauce mixture. Then put 1 cup of the ricotta cheese mixture on top of that, then another 2 noodles. Next put another cup of the meat and tomato sauce mixture down, and the rest of the ricotta cheese mixture on top of that. Put the last 3 dry lasagna noodles down and top with remaining meat and tomato sauce mixture and any remaining mozzarella cheese. Cover the baking dish with foil and bake for 45 minutes. Remove the foil and bake for 15 minutes more or until the cheese on top is turning slightly brown. Serve with lots of parmesan cheese.

Lou's Campfire Hot Dogs

Lou and camping just don't go together, but for Katie's sake she pretends she likes camping. Lou is a great pretender, and her tendency to not be herself always lands her in a heap of trouble-this time notwithstanding. So even though Lou is not a big fan of camping or the great outdoors, she takes Katie on what she envisions will be a memorable mother daughter nature trip and ends up not only spraining her ankle, but also getting into a huge fight with Katie. Luckily for Lou, though the camping trip is a bit of a disaster, she has this recipe which was handed down to her by Tim which is simple but stellar: Hot dogs with baked beans ON the hotdogs. We have imagined them a bit fancier-like the famous Montreal hot dog-not just a plain hot dog with a can of baked beans slapped on top, but if you want to go the simple route, you won't be disappointed. Even the queen of over complexity herself (Lou) likes them like that after all!

Serves 4

Ingredients:

- 1 package of hotdogs
- 1 bag of hot dog buns
- 1 can of baked beans
- Optional extra toppings:

- 1 cup of coleslaw
- ½ cup onion, chopped
- ½ cup of relish

1. Start a wood fire in an open fire pit. Open a can of baked beans and heat the beans by carefully placing the opened can in some hoat embers near the edge of your fire. While this is heating, open the package of hotdogs and place each on a metal skewer and cook until the edge of each hotdog starts to split a bit and get browned.

2. Place eat hotdog in a hot dog bun and top with baked beans and the optional toppings too if desired.

CHAPTER 4:
DESSERTS
& BEVERAGES

Maggie's Saskatoon Berry Pie

Saskatoon berries are as Canadian as berries come. Also called Service berries, they are native to the Canadian Prairies and are one of the rare fruits that grow wild in Canada in areas where most fruits and vegetables cannot grow because of the short growing season (i.e. the Saskatoon berry bush is hardy to negative 50 degrees Celsius, yes, most of Canada is very cold!). Saskatoon berries taste like blueberries that have been crossed with apples so you can imagine it's a perfect berry for a pie. Being such a common berry in Canada, it's no surprise that Saskatoon berry pie is so popular in Canada. It is also Tim's son Shane's favorite type of pie and everytime he comes to Heartland he makes it a point to stop at Maggie's to pick up some of this delicious pie.

Ingredients:

- ¼ cup sugar
- 3 Tablespoons of flour
- 4 cups of Saskatoon berries

- 2 Tablespoons of lemon juice
- ¼ cup butter
- 2 store bought pie crusts

1. Preheat your own to 350 degrees F/220 degrees C. Put the Saskatoon berries in a large pot of water and heat over high heat for about 10 minutes. Next, add the lemon juice, then the sugar and the flour. You can also add a little cornstarch (about 1 teaspoon) to thicken up the mixture as well.

2. Pour the berry mixture into one of the pie trusts and dot with the butter, about a pat of butter dotted around on the berry mixture. Cover with top crust and seal the edges together. Flute the edges by pressing down with your thumb all along the seam of the pie.

3. Cover the pie crust with foil and Bake for 35 minutes, then uncover the pie and bake another 10-15 minutes or until the top pie crust starts to turn a bit light brown.

Lou's Fancy Microwave Brownies

Even though Lou becomes somewhat of a food aficionado, she is still a very busy mom who wears multiple hats and often doesn't have enough time to make dinner, or at least fuss around with dessert! So we imagine that to make brownies as she often does, she must resort to using the old microwave! This might not sound great, but brownies are one dessert that lend themselves very well to being made in the microwave, and making brownies the quick and easy way would leave Lou plenty of time to gather the toppings for her brownies, this is still Lou after all, and we would never expect Lou to eat or serve brownies in any other way than 'fancy'.

Believe it or not though, using a microwave to make brownies is the fastest way to serve 'fancy brownies' that both look beautiful and taste delicious!

Ingredients

- 2 eggs
- 1 cup sugar
- ½ cup butter, softened
- 2 teaspoons vanilla extract
- 1 cup flour

- ½ cup unsweetened cocoa powder or if you use sweetened only use ½ cup sugar
- ½ teaspoon baking powder
- ¼ teaspoon salt
- ½ cup walnuts, chopped

1. The easiest way to make these brownies is to use a food processor to mix all the ingredients, but if you don't have one, you can just mix everything by hand. Mix together the eggs, sugar, butter and vanilla extract and beat for about a minute or until creamy.

2. Next, add the flour, unsweetened or sweetened cocoa powder, baking powder and salt and mix it all together.

3. Lastly put in the walnuts and fold them into the brownie batter. Line a glass or ceramic 8 inch round or square pan with parchment paper or spray your pan with nonstick cooking spray. Microwave on high for 4 minutes if you have a microwave with 1000 wattage or more, if under you can microwave for 5 minutes.

Georgie's Famous Author Cupcakes

When Lou goes away on a book tour Georgie first feels at loose ends but quickly gets busy and happier when she dives right into the daily life of the busy Heartland ranch. Still she manages (with the help of Youtube we're sure!) to make these cupcakes to celebrate Lou's homecoming from her book tour. Like Georgie herself we imagine her cupcakes would be sweet but a little rough around the edges. This recipe makes about 12 cupcakes so Georgie could write AUTHOR twice if she wanted to!

Ingredients:

- 1 cup flour
- 2 eggs
- ½ cup sugar
- ½ cup sweetened cocoa powder
- ⅓ cup oil
- 2 teaspoon vanilla extract
- ½ cup buttermilk
- 1 teaspoon of baking powder
- ½ teaspoon baking soda

- Frosting:
- 1 stick of unsalted butter
- 2 cups of powdered sugar
- ½ cup milk
- 1 teaspoon of vanilla extract
- ½ cup unsweetened cocoa powder
- Pinch of salt
- Optional: pink food coloring

Instructions:

1. Place cupcake liners in a muffin tin with 12 cups in it. Next, preheat the oven to 350. To make the cupcakes mix the dry ingredients in a large mixing bowl: flour, cocoa powder, baking powder, baking soda, and salt. Now mix the eggs, oil, buttermilk and vanilla into the dry ingredients until mixed. Pour the mixture into the cupcake liners. Each cupcake liner should be about half full of the mixture.

2. Bake in the preheated oven for 20-25 minutes or until a toothpick inserted into the center of one of the cupcakes comes out clean. To make the frosting mix all these ingredients in a blender or with an electric mixer: unsalted butter, powdered sugar, milk, vanilla extract and salt. Take out about ½ cup of the frosting in a small mixing bowl and add 5 drops of pink food coloring to it and stir. Add the cocoa powder to the remaining frosting and mix for an additional minute. Frost the cupcakes once cooled with the chocolate frosting and use the pink frosting to write 'Author' or whatever else you like, like Heartland!

Vegan La Bete Noire: The Black Beast

There's no doubt that Lou is besides herself upset that her ex Mitch not only had a new girlfriend Maya but that Maya is invited over for dinner to the Heartland ranch-and on top of all that, Maya is a Vegan. However, Lou wasn't about to let a heart wrenching situation like this get in the way of her making a fabulous vegan dinner for Mitch's girlfriend that is sure to wow-when all Lou probably really wants to do is punch both Mitch and Maya's lights out. Though we don't know exactly what Lou made for dessert for this Vegan dinner, it's easy to imagine that making a dessert called The Black Beast would be something Lou would make and might also be calling Maya in her mind, and unlike Lou's attitude at the Vegan dinner, this dessert is sweet and beautiful.

Ingredients:

Crust:

- 2 cups almond pieces
- ¼ cup flour

- 4 Tablespoons vegan butter (like soy butter which is really easy to find at local grocery stores)
- ¼ cup brown sugar

Cake:

- 1 16 ounce bag of semisweet or bittersweet
- chocolate chips
- ½ cup vegan butter
- 1 block of tofu, (14 ounces)
- 2 Tablespoons cornstarch

- Ganache Topping:
- 1 cup soy (or almond) milk
- 1 bag of semisweet chocolate chips (12 ounces)
- 1 block of silken tofu

Making the crust: Toast the almonds in a frying pan over medium high heat. Stir constantly. Once the almonds are light brown, place on a paper towel lined plate. After they have cooled a bit transfer them to a food processor or blender to blend them into tiny bits. Next, mix the almond with the flour, butter, and brown sugar. Spread this mixture over the bottom of a spring form 8 or 9 inch springform pan and place in the refrigerator to chill.

Making the cake: Preheat your oven to 350 degrees F. Whisk the coffee and sugar until the sugar dissolves. Add the chocolate and butter until they both melt together. Pour the mixture into a food processor or blender. Add the cornstarch and tofu and puree until all combined. Cook for 30 minutes in the oven.

Making the Ganache: Pour the soy (or almond) milk into a pan and cook over medium heat until it starts to simmer. Remove it from the heat and add teh chocolate chips and stir until they all melt.

To assemble the cake, layer the cake on top of the crust and then pour the ganache over that. Chill for about 1 hour before serving.

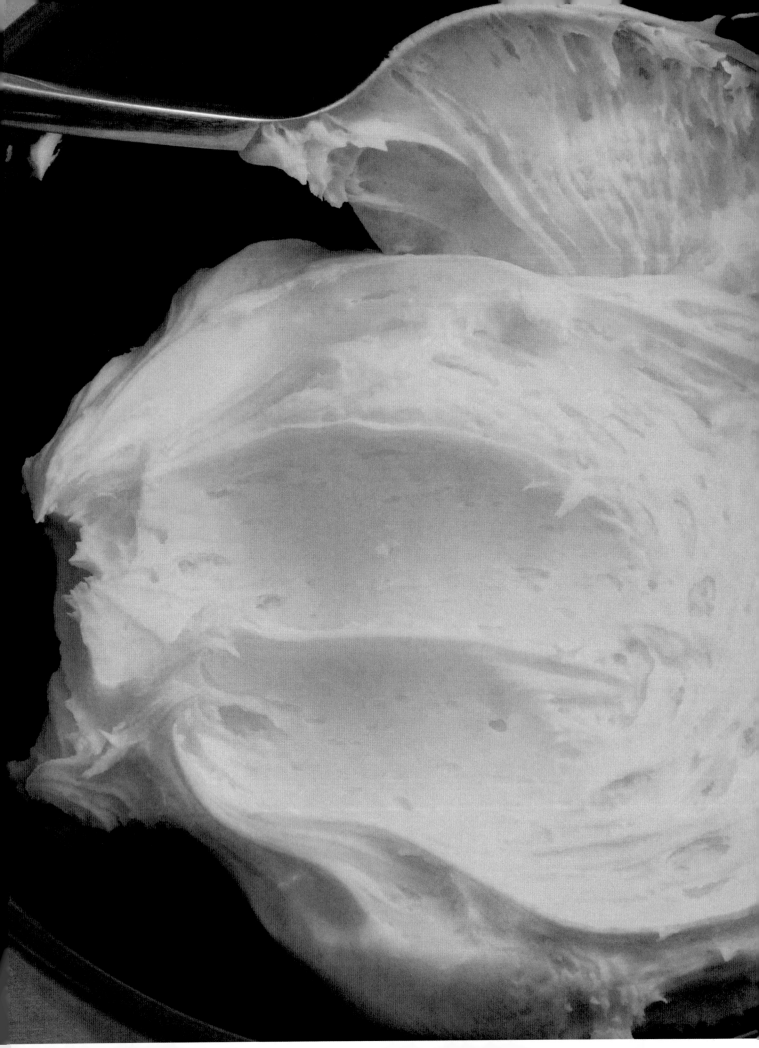

Amy's Simple but Beautiful Vanilla Cake & Frosting

Out of everyone in the Heartland family, the one person who never cooks much is Amy. It seems it's not just because she's busy treating horses, but also because it just doesn't seem like her forte. Like the time she tried to make a cake for Ty's birthday. It took her several attempts to get a simple vanilla birthday cake right, but Ty was still very touched by the amount of effort she took in making it, especially because it appears he knows she is not one for cooking and baking. True to form then, we imagine that though she could have easily just used store bought frosting as Lou did for Grandpa Jack's birthday cakes, makes not only the cake herself but the frosting too. The frosting is not very difficult to make after all, and is more of Amy's style, simple but beautiful.

Ingredients:

Cake:

- ½ cup white sugar
- 1 teaspoon baking soda
- 1 teaspoon lemon juice
- ¼ cup canola oil

- 1 teaspoon vanilla extract
- 1 cup water
- 1 cup flour

Frosting:

- 1 pint whipping cream
- 1 cup powdered sugar

- 1 teaspoon vanilla extract
- ¼ teaspoon salt

1. Cake: Preheat the oven to 180C/350F. Mix the dry ingredients in a mixing bowl. Mix the wet ingredients in another mixing bowl. Now mix them together and pour into two parchment or shortening lined 6 inch round cake pans. Place in the oven for 20-25 minutes. Cool before frosting.

2. Frosting: Place the whipping cream into a mixing bowl and beat until it becomes bubbly and frothy. Next start adding the powdered sugar slowly, a tablespoon at a time. Then add the salt and vanilla extract. Keep beating the cream until it forms stiff peaks.

Tim's Favorite Apple Pie

Tim Fleming is a royal pain in the Bartlett family and being a royal pain he often expects to be treated like royalty. Case in point is when he is shot by cattle rustlers in Season 3 and decides to stay at the Heartland Ranch to recuperate. True to his character, Tim expects everyone to wait on him hand and foot-including driving to Maggie's Diner to get him some Vegetarian Chili (recipe on page 35) and some of their equally famous Apple Pie. Though Amy and Lou are very gracious in catering to Tim's every whim, his constant need to be waited on grates on Grandpa Jack's nerves. When Tim asks for a piece of cheese to accompany his pie, Grandpa Jack seems like his head will explode! We have to agree with Tim on this one though..this Apple Macaroon Pie is delicious with a slice of cheddar cheese and is fit for a King, or a royal pain in the....

Makes 1 Pie

Ingredients:

- 9 inch/22.8 cm unbaked pie crust (just make your life easier and buy a frozen pie crust!)

- 4 cups Granny Smith apples, thinly sliced

- ¾ cup sugar

- 3 tbsp flour

- ½ tsp salt

- 1 tsp cinnamon

- 1 egg

- 3 tbsp butter, melted

- 1 cup sweetened coconut flakes

1. Preheat the oven to 350 degrees F/ degrees C. Place the slightly thawed unbaked pie crust on top of a cookie sheet and bake it on the middle rack of the oven for 10 minutes. While it is baking, mix together the sliced apples, ½ cup sugar, 2 tbsp of flour, the cinnamon and salt in a large mixing bowl. Pour these ingredients into the partially baked pie crust. Place aluminum foil over the top of the pie so the crust doesn't start to brown too quickly and place back in the oven for 30 minutes.

2. While this is baking, combine the 1 egg, ¼ cup sugar, 1 tbsp of flour, the butter and the sweetened coconut flakes in a large mixing bowl. Pour this mixture over the apple pie and bake for another 20 minutes uncovered with the aluminum foil.

Maggie's German Tourists Favorite Peach Pie

The secret to a perfect peach pie is selecting perfect peaches. Ones sold in grocery stores are often picked before ripe, then refrigerated at a low temperature; the result is a hard, mealy peach. Mrs Bell's 'Madison' variety peach tree produces some of the sweetest peaches on the planet. A Madison is the princess of peaches, and not suitable for long transport to market. Try buying your peaches from a farmers market, or truck stand. Select dark yellow fruit with a hint of pretty red peachy color, which indicates it ripened on the tree. Ripe peaches will greet you with a sweet aroma, and are usually round. But, too ripe and your pie will become peach soup. Gently press & your peach should feel soft, but will not easily bruise. Ask when the peaches were picked; 1 to 3 days is ideal.

Ingredients:

- 1 1/4 cups sugar
- 1/3 cup all purpose flour
- 1 teaspoon cinnamon
- 1/2 teaspoon nutmeg
- 1/8 teaspoon salt
- 2 pounds, or 8 medium, or 6 cups; peeled & sliced fresh freestone peaches. Select peaches that

- are firm, and ripe. Avoid bruised & mushy peaches.
- 2 Tablespoons fresh lemon juice
- 3 Tablespoon butter, cut into pieces
- 1 egg
- 1 Tablespoon coarse sugar crystals

1. For filling: In a bowl; mix sugar, flour, cinnamon, and nutmeg, and salt.In a large bowl, slice peaches, then sprinkle & toss with lemon juice.Gently stir dry ingredients into peaches. Pour peaches into the prepared bottom pie crust, dot with butter. Cover with top crust, then flute & seal edges.

2. Cut several slits to vent. Beat 1 Tablespoon water into egg & brush over top crust, sprinkle coarse sugar crystals over crust.

3. Bake approx 1 hour & 15 minutes until the filling is hot & bubbling. Cover with foil if the crust browns too quickly during baking.

Grandma Lyndy's Deep Dish Rhubarb & Blueberry Custard Pie

Custard fruit pies are easy to make, and add a richness to your favorite fruit pie filling.

Tart fruits like rhubarb blended into a sweet custard, create a sweet & sour complexity, plain fruit pies cannot achieve. Many claim the popular strawberry Rhubarb pie cannot compete with this old farmhouse favorite. Lyndy's mother Louise created this recipe, using only rhubarb. Louise served it at Jack & Lyndy's engagement party, and it soon became Jack's favorite pie. After Lyndy set up her own kitchen at Heartland Ranch, she didn't quite have enough rhubarb one day, and added a cup of blueberries. Jack liked it so well, Lyndy added rhubarb / blueberry pie to her recipe box. Rhubarb and blueberries are rich in antioxidants, high in fiber, and are both 'superfoods'.

Makes 1 Pie

Ingredients:

Buy 2 refrigerated pie crusts

- A glass 10" deep pie dish is required.

- Preheat oven to 375 degrees.

Ingredients:

- 3 eggs
- 3 Tbsp. whole milk, (or almond, soy, etc)
- 1 3/4 to 2 cups granulated sugar
- 4 Tbsp. all-purpose flour, (or gf equivalent)
- 2 dash's cinnamon, (1/4 teas)

- 1 teas vanilla
- 6 cups fresh rhubarb (rinsed with ends cut off)
- 1 generous cup fresh (rinsed & de-stemmed) or frozen blueberries

1. Preheat oven to 375 degrees. Beat: eggs, milk, sugar, flour, cinnamon, & vanilla in a large bowl till well blended. Set aside. Cut rhubarb into 1 inch pieces. Gently stir blueberries into rhubarb; Saskatoon berries may be substituted. Pour fruit into custard and mix well, being certain all the fruit is coated with custard.

2. Fill prepared bottom pastry crust with custard & fruit mixture. Cover with top pastry crust & follow pie crust recipe to finish. Bake 375 degrees for one hour or more, until the crust is golden brown, and the filling begins to bubble through slits in crust. Refrigerate after 2 days.

Mrs. Bell's Relaxing Herbal Tea

One of the most iconic characters on Heartland, Mrs. Bell loves to grow flowers and herbs in her many gardens. She also loves to cook with her own fruits and vegetables as when she makes her famous strawberry jam and she also uses many of the herbs she grows to make relaxing teas.

One herb she uses is ironically called horsemint and she garnishes it with an edible flower that grows wild on the Alberta Prairie called Linden flowers. Like Mrs. Bell herself, this tea is both sweet and nourishing. Another benefit of this herbal tea is that it can relax even the most anxious of people, like Lou, and if this tea is drunk regularly is sure to make you 'as healthy as a horse!'

Makes 3 cups of Tea

Ingredients:

- ½ cup of Horsemint leaves
- Tea Infuser or strainer
- Handful of Linden flowers
- 3 cups of Water

1. Boil 3 cups of water in a medium size pan and drop the tea infuser stuffed full of the horsemint into it. If you don't want to use a tea infuser you can simply drop the horsemint leaves right into the water.

2. Boil for a full five minutes until the smell of the horsemint starts to fill the room. Then drop the Linden flowers into the water and boil for another minute. Strain the mixture in a metal colander and pour the remaining liquid into a mug.

Maggie's Strawberry Milkshake

In one of the early seasons of Heartland, Amy's best friend tells Caleb that if she's ever feeling low she makes herself a big strawberry milkshake. We wholeheartedly agree that downing a delicious and fragrant strawberry creamy milkshake makes everything better! If you don't have ice cream you can always use frozen yogurt or regular yogurt, just make sure to add some extra honey or a bit of sugar to keep that sweet milkshake flavor. Also, if you use frozen strawberries use a little less ice cream and a little more milk or it will be super thick. Anyways this milkshake is so good it's easy to see why it's a favorite of many on Maggie's menu.

Makes 2 Milkshakes

Ingredients:

- 2 scoops of vanilla ice cream, about ¾ cup
- 1 cup of milk

- 1 cup of strawberries, tops removed
- 1 teaspoon of honey

Pinch of salt

1. Put all ingredients into a blender and blend for about 1 minute or until smooth.

Maggie's Famous Coffee
(with Grandpa Jack's Special Add-Ins)

Maggie's is one of the most popular places in Hudson for the locals like Jack, Nick Harwell, Val Stanton and Caleb to grab a quick cup of coffee. Though several times Maggie's has considered getting a fancy coffee machine it appears most Hudson locals enjoy a simple cup of well brewed strong coffee. No double espresso skim chai lattes here! Of course Grandpa Jack being the good ole' Canadian guy that he is, enjoys his coffee with a few additional special add-ins namely Canadian maple syrup and a little splash of 'the good stuff.

Makes 1 Cup of Coffee

Ingredients:

- 1 tablespoon maple syrup (Canadian of course!)

- 1 cup of black coffee made double strength

- Optional add: splash to ¼ cup whiskey

1. Pour the maple syrup and whiskey into a heated glass and mix. Next, pour in hot double strength coffee. To make double strength coffee you make coffee in preferably your old fashioned coffee machine and then instead of pouring water into the percolator you pour in the coffee you just made and it will come out double strength.

About the Authors

Nita Abbott is no stranger to the foodie world and loves Heartland, the country life, cooking and eating comfort food alike. She lives in New England with her dogs, chickens and human family.
You can follow Nita on Facebook at https://m.facebook.com/groups/keepheartlandstrong and on her Youtube channel at: https://youtube.com/c/AlwaysInMyHeartHeartland

Mike Hurley comes from a family of storytellers and childhood memories of his father and uncles spinning yarns during family meals captivated his young imagination. Today, Mike is an avid writer of Heartland fanfiction. Also a long time beekeeper and home cook, Mike finds solace with his bees and loves to create delicious honey and recipes along with his wife Priscilla. Mike lives in Colorado with his wife, three small dogs, and several horses. You can also follow Mike's Heartland fanfiction journey on WattPad at Mikehurleytamy.

US/Metric Conversion Chart

Volume Conversions
U.S. Volume..Metric

¼ cup	60 mm
⅓ cup	90 mm
½ cup	125 mm
⅔ cup	160 mm
¾ cup	180 mm
1 cup	250 mm
1 pint	500 mm
1 quart	1 liter

Weight Conversions
U.S. Weight..Metric

¼ pound	115 grams
½ pound	225 grams
¾ pound	340 grams
1 pound	454 grams

US/Metric Conversion Chart

Oven Temperature Conversions
Fahrenheit...Celsius

350 degrees F	180 degrees C
375 degrees F	190 degrees C
400 degrees F	205 degrees C
425 degrees F	220 degrees C
450 degrees F	230 degrees C

Baking Pan Sizes
U.S. Sizes...Metric

9 x 1 ½ inch round baking pan	23 x 3.5 cm cake tin
11 x 7 x 1 ½ inch baking pan	28 x 18 x 4 cm baking tin
13 x 9 x 2 inch baking pan	30 x 20 x 5 cm baking tin
2 quart rectangular baking pan	30 x 20 x 5 cm baking tin
15 x 10 x 2 inch baking pan	30 x 20 x 2 cm baking tin
9 inch pie plate	22 x 13 x 7 cm or 2 lb narrow loa

Made in the USA
Middletown, DE
23 August 2024

59647753R10071